# Clicker Training for Fun with Horses

Quick tips to improve

your results & relationship

with your horse

**Clicker Training for Fun with Horses**

Bright Spot Publishing

ISBN 9781480298187

©2012 Kimberley Freeman

World Clicker Equine Games Top 5 Clicker Trainer

videos at
http://horseclickerfun.blogspot.com

# Horse Training Tips

## How to click with your horse

**Creating an Alphabet**

Clicker work is more than a training tool: it's a way of communicating with horses, opening the floodgates for equine learning while a creating a stronger bond with your horse.

There's nothing magic about the clicker itself. It's simply a device that makes a distinct, sharp sound, marking the exact second the horse did something right. It's the timing of the click that's key: after all, the tool is only as good as the hand holding it.

The joy of clicker training is that it's the beginning of a personal conversation with your horse. You are building a vocabulary together. And once they've learned the basic ABCs, you can teach them just about anything.

Within days, you have a horse who becomes engaged in the learning process even if after being dulled from a life of being dictated to. Even a horse who was "broken" (learned to obey to avoid pain and discomfort) can be "woken" as a learner.

Work for horses (and humans) is always more enjoyable when you get to make decisions and explore options.

It's always a thrill to see the light bulb go on when a horse gets the connection between behavior, click and treat. It's this moment that opens the door to a horse who perks up when he sees you, prefers your company to other horses, and looks to you to for direction, asking, "Hey! What's next?"

**Building Bridges**
In the world of operant conditioning, the clicker is formally known as a "bridge tool." Basically, you're bridging between behavior and reward while building a bridge between your mind and your horse's.

Think of the click as a promise marker that says, "**Good job! A treat is on the way.**"

Clicker training began in the 1970s with dolphins but has since been adapted for training dogs and horses. Zoos are even using it now to persuade chimps, otters, giraffes and even crocodiles to take voluntary injections.

In clicker training, the horse is part of the team. He has choices and gets to make decisions. He's encouraged to explore, think and "solve the puzzle." He is not punished for doing something wrong—other than being ignored. Soon he learns that only requested or desired behavior "works." He is essentially earning his food, which as a nice byproduct, also happens to earn you respect in his eyes.

**Crossing the bridge**
After the bridge is conditioned, it can be used to train new behaviors with more detailed techniques such as capturing, free shaping, observational learning, successive approximation, and micro-shaping.

For now, this is the basic sequence of events:

**Behavior → BRIDGE → reinforcer**

...in other words,

**action →CLICK → treat**

For consistent communication, the bridging stimulus or CLICK should be given the same way each time. Lindsay Wood studied the efficacy of bridging types (2008) and found that a clicker was more effective than a verbal bridge due to the precise, unmistakable sound.

**Trigger Finger**
Beware of your own enthusiasm. Sometimes you may find it tempting to CLICK repeatedly as a sort of jackpot DING-DING-DING (i.e., multiple clicks in a row) but this is not advisable. Studies show repeating the click only marks multiple behaviors that occurred after the first one, (Stafford, 2007) which can lead to confusion.

The reinforcer (treat) itself can be multiplied as a jackpot for an excellent effort or performance, but the bridge should remain single in each execution. Three pieces of carrot in a row while you sing their praises gets the message across very clearly.

**DING-DING-DING!**
The bridge is the cue that tells the horse "YES, you got it right that second. Reward coming up." When choosing what type of bridge to use, the main objective is to select something distinct, precise, and easily discernable to the horse. A precise signal (such as a clicker) has proven to be more effective than a spoken word.

It is important to choose a distinct sound only used to mark behavior and never used any other way. Beware of using only a verbal word as a bridge. The horse hears us talk all day. Words run together, plus each trainer will have a different tone and voice inflection.

In advanced work, very subtle cues are paired with the clicker then clicker is faded out, shifting to a visual only. An example of an unusual bridge is told by Grey Stafford in his book, *Zoomility* (2007), in which a dog trainer pushed her glasses up on her nose (as the click/bridge) in the show ring to communicate with her dog in a place where overt reinforcement was not allowed.

So whether you prefer whistles to clickers or

visual cues over auditory, any signal can be used as long as the horse can perceive it easily and it has been conditioned as a bridging stimulus.

**How to condition a bridge**
Once the type of bridge has been selected, it needs to be conditioned. Think of this as teaching the animal a common language. You have to speak the same language before you can communicate. If he/she doesn't understand what the bridge means, the signal will be meaningless and only cause confusion.

Conditioning the bridge is simply associating the bridging stimulus (click sound) with a primary reinforcer (yummy snack).

NOTE: Remember a bridge is only as strong as the reinforcement treat it's linked with, so use choose something they really like. If you're out of their favorite goody, dole out the morning's grain ration a little at a time. Even if they prefer treats to their usual grain or pellets, when they're hungry, anything edible is motivating.

**Loading the Clicker**
If you are starting with a new horse who has never heard a clicker, begin by free feeding several reinforcement foods. Take note of which he prefers so you can later reward accordingly.

Make sure your first few session are with the

horse contained somewhere so you can step away if he gets pushy. When he looks away, click and treat. Once you have shaped him to be polite, you can move on to targeting.

Present a target between you and the horse: a tennis ball on a stick, a halter, a cone; anything your horse can safely touch with his nose. Hold it still in a convenient place and DO NOT chase him with it or push it closer. Let him come to it.

When he moves toward it, bumps it or makes the slightest motion to sniff at it, CLICK and treat in quick succession. Use a small amount (i.e., tiny bites rather huge portions) so the horse can finish each bite quickly and does not get overfed or full. Be sure to stop your training session before the horse is satiated.

You want to put the target item where the horse will naturally see it and be curious enough to sniff or bump it.

At first, any motion toward it gets a click/treat. Each successive attempt builds until he is intentionally touching it with his nose waiting to hear the click. You want him to be successful; so don't get ahead of yourself and start moving the target up down and all around.

Go slow and make him feel brilliant each time he makes an effort to investigate the target item. You can work on precision later. Right now, he needs to fall in love with touching a target.

One day when he escapes his pen and is headed for the road, being able to get him back by simply targeting him to a tennis ball or empty bucket could be saving his life.

We've seen un-haltered, loose horses stop in their tracks at the word Whoa from a long distance because the idea of STOP MOVING NOW had been so well clicker trained, it became automatic. It never hurts to have an emergency brake, both around the barn and when riding.

You can use just about anything for a target Just make sure it has a distinctive look that's easy for him to recognize and soft enough he won't hurt his nose or teeth if he bumps it.

**Timing is everything**
The key to good clicker training is TIMING. Delays of even a second between behavior and click can lead to confusion. If you're not getting good progress with your horse, you are probably clicking too late.

Practice your timing alone with your horse out of earshot.

Even if you've clicked with horses before, try the next exercise to make sure your timing is as good as you think it is.

**Practice first.**
Hold the clicker in one hand and a tennis ball in the other. Drop the ball and click as it hits the floor. Then click each bounce. If you can hear the splat of the ball on floor, your click was too early or too late.

11

Next, try a game with a friend. You'll find out how it feels to be the horse, which makes you a vastly better trainer. Have a friend sit on the couch with the clicker. You are standing in the center of the room. They have something they want you to do in mind and will click if you look or move the right direction. It's like a game of HOT/COLD and you should be clicked when you're getting warmer. Try it—but no talking, grinning, or nodding allowed!

You'll feel it viscerally once you've had someone click you for an action. The second you hear the click, you are hyper-aware of what you were doing that very moment—not before or after.

Your friend should click you each time you make a motion in the right direction. The action could be turning in a circle, sitting down, holding a leg up...anything. Have fun with it and you'll learn how clicking teaches from the other end of the lead line.

### IS THE CLICKER NECESSARY?
Without a bridging signal, food is hard to use around an eager, persistent horse. It becomes more of a distraction than a communication tool.

The clicker or "bridging signal" channels that eagerness into effort and performance. The clicker tool is convenient for us--and highly motivating for horses. The clear **YES** it represents accelerates the learning curve and creates happy, eager-to-work horses. If you tire of carrying a clicker, you can gradually switch over to a tongue cluck or whistle.

### Caught in the act
Seconds matter. Make sure your click captures your horse IN the act, not after. This is the biggest mistake for beginners and leads to confusion for horse AND person. An example is when you think you're rewarding horse for dropping his head, but he thinks it was for swishing a fly with his tail.

You must click **DURING** the action you want. Otherwise you are reinforcing the ceasing of the action, so keep in mind, better to click too soon than too late.

### Biting and nippy horses
If you find your horse is getting pushy for treats, go back to the beginning and put your horse in a stall where you can step away or turn your back on bad behavior. This should be the first step when you are teaching targeting. If he ever gets to the point of begging, go back and refresh his manners.

## What should I use for rewards?

Try anything small your horse loves and can consume quickly. You don't want to stand around waiting for them to chew before moving on with the lesson, so keep rewards small.

If you're using grain, keep it to about a tablespoon. Sliced carrots or apples can work well, as do breakfast cereals, sugar cubes, peppermints, and gingersnap cookies.

Reserve your horse's very favorite treat for the special moments when they make an extra good effort or have a learning breakthrough. This is called a "Jackpot moment." It's like people playing the slot machines in Vegas, but in this case, the horse did something especially good and you want to let him know, "Ding, Ding, Ding! Perfect! That was exactly right!"

After a Jackpot effort, you'll see a look of surprise and pleasure on your horse's face when you click and deliver that super-special treat or quick succession of several.

**Note: The Jackpot is the treat delivery, not the click.**

**ONLY CLICK ONCE** but then deliver special or multiple treats, make a big fuss, then end session and move on to let him know he did great! **Beware:** For some horses, asking for a behavior over and over can imply they have not gotten it right yet so they may get discouraged and lose interest.

# Rules of the Game

**1**. If you click, you must treat. Don't break the promise or you lose the power of the clicker – and your horse's trust.

**2.** If you make a mistake and click too soon or for a behavior you did not want, don't panic. You can't rewind. Just go on with training.

**3**. Don't let a mistake—yours or the horse's-- get you frustrated or upset your timing. Just keep going. If you get mad, put the clicker away.

**4.** At the end of a session, put the clicker away and make a large gesture to convey "Game Over" to the horse. Take off your treat pouch or show from a distance that your hands are empty.

**5**. If you want to express enthusiasm, increase the number of treats for a reward, not the number of clicks. Vocal praise is a good addition AFTER the click has made it clear what all the fuss is about.

**6.** End a session on a good note, even if it means going back to something basic. You always want to leave your horse feeling clever and successful. Soon you'll see his eyes light up when the clicker comes out.

## TARGET PRACTICE

Teaching a horse to target something like a tennis ball, a cone or even a bucket is a very useful tool you'll be able to use in a lot of situations. Once a horse learns the concept of "Target" you can use it for trailer loading, ground tying, obstacle training and even "stay."

Once you teach the action then pair it with the verbal command "Target!" your horse will look around for the item and go put his nose on it. Add the word, "Hold" or "Wait" while gradually increasing the time (in one-second increments) before they get the click/treat. Soon you can use the "hold" or "wait" command for many instances—and have a horse who becomes the envy of all your friends.

Your friends and family will think he's the smartest horse they ever saw. And maybe he is, but please realize you are pretty smart for learning to communicate with another species. You're especially smart for being clear about what you ask for while teaching it in a fun way.

**Suggested target items:**

    Cone or pylon
    Tennis ball on end of a stick
    Foam pool noodle
    Hula hoop
    Halter
    Empty water bottle
    Squeaky toy

## BACK UP

It's very important in the early stages of clicker training to show the horse that the best way to get the human "vending machine" to work is by stepping away from it. It's key for him to learn that "mugging for treats" won't earn a thing and could even end the fun food game.

If you have a pushy horse, putting "back up" on the clicker menu is a super way to teach good manners and keep your kids—and toes-- safe.

Start with your horse in a stall or behind a fence. If he gets excited when you first introduce the food treats, simply step back to keep yourself out of reach or turn your back if he mouths your hand or treat bag. This is the consequence. Horses learn consequences of their actions very quickly.

Keep this in mind as you let the horse explore and he's going to discover that going directly to the vending machine and pushing on it never earns a treat. It might even make it disappear.

He's learning he never gets clicked or treated for sniffing fingers, nuzzling, licking, pulling on arms, nudging, bumping or pushing adults of children.

## Head Down
This is a useful skill for any horse and allows you to be able to calm them in stressful situations and also comes in handy so children can safely halter, bridle and lead a horse.

Begin teaching the head down cue by placing your hand on your horse's neck, just behind his ears. RESIST the urge push down--just let the weight of your hand rest on his mane but imagine your hand as totally fixed in space in time.

Keep it totally still even if you feel a slight acceptance or drop. Do not go down with him—you're teaching him to drop away from the slightest suggestion of pressure!

Moving away from pressure is always the right answer and this will be a goldmine when you start riding him and guiding with your legs.

If at first, his head goes up instead of down, gently stay with him until he finds the right answer. Once he drops his head, he finds the release (right answer) so quickly click and treat.

You may find that your horse wants to bring his head right back up again. The reason for this is he doesn't feel safe leaving his head low where he can't see the horizon line, so his head pops right back up again this is totally normal when he's going to hold his head down from more than a few seconds, he is saying "I am turning over responsibility of watching out for predators to you. I trust you to keep me safe."

These three exercises (**TARGET, BACK UP, HEAD DROP**) are the basic building blocks for many fun and useful things to come.

Clicker trained horses feel free to have fun and are a joy to work with—and all you need is a bag of carrots and a clicker.

## TROUBLESHOOTING

### "What should I do if my horse leaves or does something wrong?"

Just pause and reassess. Were you gong too fast for him and he lost interest in the game? Did you hear him grumble "no fun" as he left?

Each task needs to be easily achieved and you should set things up for his success. Make it easy for him to choose the right action. It's not a test, it's you teaching him to relax and explore. You're there to guide him, not correct him. Show him it's safe to explore and make mistakes. Set up the task to make it easy for him to be successful.

When he's being quickly reinforced for correct responses, he'll understand what you want and offer more and more.

### Stuck?

Got a confused horse with a sudden case of ELI (Equine Lost Interest)?

First, make sure you're only training one criterion at a time. Humans often demand too much, too soon. An example: If you want a horse to back straight and fast, chunk your training down into small steps and focus on one small element of the behavior at a time. Raise your standards in small increments so the horse can continue to be successful.

If your horse gets confused or loses interest in training, he's telling you he needs to have the task broken down into smaller steps or needs more frequent breaks. Pawing is generally a sign of frustration or being overwhelmed.

**Try to keep sessions under 5 minutes each.** You should stop while he's still into it: don't wear out your welcome. If he wants more, give him a few minutes break: do something else that's mundane with no pressure, then see if he follows you around asking for more games.

**Onward and upward**
Once a certain behavior is established—but NOT perfected—you should switch from a fixed schedule of reinforcement to a variable reinforcement schedule. A fixed schedule means the horse is rewarded with a click and snack every time he offers a behavior.

When you're first teaching a new behavior, you want to keep the rate of reinforcement HIGH AND FAST so a fixed schedule is necessary. Once a learned behavior is getting steady and consistent with a correct response 8 out of 10 times, it's time to switch to a variable reinforcement schedule to perfect it.

This means you're not going to reinforce every effort anymore. Your horse will start experimenting to see if he can get his vending machine to work again. Watch closely and pick and choose the best examples of the behavior you're looking for. It might be every third or fifth try.

This is the biggest mistake new horse owners make: not weaning the horse off of "every effort gets a treat every time." Taken to extreme, your horse could get dull and bored with the routine. Why should he try hard when a half-hearted attempt still earns a cookie? You need to keep him guessing a little to keep his interest up and mind sharp.

Ask him to stand still three seconds longer, or hold that neck slightly more arched. Whatever tweak you want to shape, a variable reinforcement rate will get you there.

**BE PATIENT AND KIND**
Think of a horse during learning time as a child with stage fright performing in public. She may be able to recite lines perfectly at home, but in front of an audience, she frets and forgets everything.

A horse in training is the same way. Treat your horse with the same kindness and consideration you would give a frightened child—even if they don't seem frightened, they can become frustrated in a second, so be patient.

If a behavior you thought was learned deteriorates, go back to a previous step in the shaping process the horse understood well. It's like starting over in reciting the alphabet when you get lost at H-I-J-K. Just return to a point where your horse was successful and rebuild from there.

**TRY A DIFFERENT APPROACH**
If a shaping procedure is not creating progress, think up a new way to ask for the desired behavior. If he does not understand what you're asking, try asking another way.

**Body Language**
Do not wear sunglasses when working with horses. They need to see your expression and your eyes tell them a lot. Horses read our intent from our eyes as well as our bodies, our expression, the way we face them, move towards or away from them.

Watch how a lead mare faces and confronts a fractious colt, then how she turns away when he's forgiven. Staring intently is pressure. For a herd/prey animal, a stare can feel like they're being sized up for dinner by a predator. For a horse, looking away is a welcome release of pressure. Release of pressure equals reward.

Keep in mind the courtesies of communication in HorseWorld and you'll get way more respect for knowing their language.

**Stubbornness**
If you think your horse is stubborn, he may just be resistant. You might be, too if someone was making odd demands of you with no clear reason. Remember, 99% of resistance is just your horse's way of

communicating he's fearful or doesn't understand something.

**Negative Reinforcers**

Negative reinforcers are essentially punishment and part of the old-school cowboy days of breaking horses. These days, we want to fix horses, not break them. Whips should only be used as an extension of our arm for guidance, not pain.

People who lunge horses in a circle with a whip poised behind the horse's hindquarters are basically nagging and micromanaging their horses.

Imagine if you were at work and your boss was following you around with a cattle prod, watching your every move. If you slow down for lunch, BAM! No matter what you do, that prod is poised at your butt to strike. Would you be productive? Would you like your boss? Or would you start to resent and eventually ignore him?

If you feel you must hold a whip, the horse needs to understand it's not there to intimidate but to offer clues to what you're asking for. Keep the tip parked on the ground and only pick it when necessary. Never snap a horse with the lash. The best "whips" are merely sticks with a string added for reach and motion, not elastic sting.

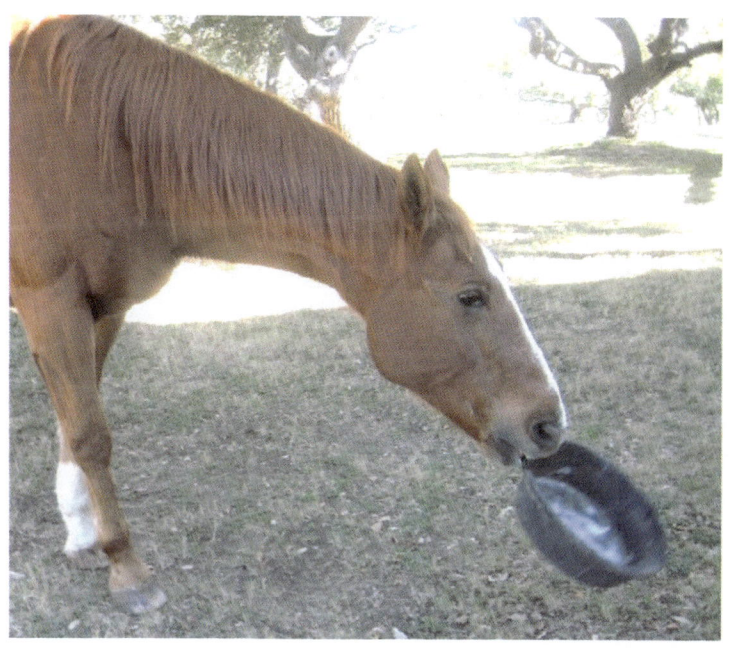

**DINNER TIME!**
Only a subordinate horse gives up his food to another. Keep this in mind when feeding your horse. He'll be super alert at feeding time, and in your horse's eyes, you are setting a standard here.

You see the transaction as an act of love. A chance to nourish your horse with quality food that will make him shiny and healthy. He sees it as a lower herd member turning over valuable resources to him.

To avoid confusing things, feeding time needs to be consistent. Think of it as training time, because everything you do around your horse is training for good or bad. When it comes to a pile of grain in a bucket, he needs to feel he earned it, whether it' training time or dinnertime.

Even if you're in a hurry to feed, take 5 seconds to at least ask for a quiet contained head position or a polite back up.

Otherwise, if you waltz up and present him a pile of free food, it's like you saying, **"I GIVE THIS UP TO YOU, YOUR HIGHNESS!** You are above me and eat first while I stand aside and watch with nothing."

Feeding time is the perfect chance to brush up a previous clicker session. Ask for a two-step back up. Or a head drop. Anything your horse learned recently, now is the ideal time test it. Even it's something small, your horse is earning his food, not taking it from a subordinate member of his herd. If you really want your horse looking up to you, use the clicker to teach him teach him he can only begin eating his breakfast/dinner once you give permission.

Horses are not like dogs, but they do have a strong herd mentality in terms of pecking order. At the top is the alpha mare. Every horse knows who stands where at all times.

Watch a herd of horses. They chose their leaders every day. Pecking order can occasionally shift within the ranks, but generally the top horse stays at the top unharmed. That's where you want to be. And keep in mind; the horse on the lower end of the ladder probably sees you as a way moving up.

**What did horse number 11 in the pecking order say when his human stepped through the gate? "Here comes number 12."**

Once you fall below a horse in terms of respect and leadership, you are essentially agreeing to getting pushed around, ignored, stomped, bitten or chased, just as any other horse of lower ranking gets from the others every
day

**Whoa vs. No**
When you're working with your horse, be careful not to fall into dog training mode. Never use the word NO as in "Don't do that" and do not use the word WHOA unless you

want all four feet to stop moving immediately.

In fact, avoid the word NO completely. To a horse, it sounds identical to WHOA. If he nips you and you say NO! he thinks it just means to keep his feet still—but it's okay to bite you. If you yell NO and try to slap him, he just learns to be faster than you. If your horse does something that cannot be ignored, say a specific word. QUIT! Is good because it is short, sharp and does not sound anything else.

Think of Whoa like the old game of "freeze." The horse should understand it means stop all movement NOW. When you use the WHOA word, you want to count on it the first time, every time.

**LOOK OUT!**
Horses feel safer with their head up high enough to scan the horizon for predators or any unusual, suspect movement. Lowering their head to graze generally means they've relaxed or feel comfortable knowing another herd member is in charge of "lookout."

If your horse is alone, the best favor you can do is to make him feel safe. Scan the horizon for him while he eats—especially if the two of you are away from home in a new place. Look around and put yourself between him and any commotion. Think of yourself as the lead stallion or mare keeping the family safe.

YOU know there are no mountain lions out there, but he doesn't. Keep a lookout, even if it's just for roving plastic bags in the wind. Your horse will see you as a trusted friend and you win big points.

Another way to earn big points is to go out and survey grassy areas beyond your horse's pen or pasture. Know how to spot his very favorite kind of grass or weeds. Now that you know the "best places in town" take him "out to dinner." Halter him and immediately take him directly that favorite patch of grass across the street or down the road.

Point it out or tear a hunk yourself and give the "OKAY" or AT EASE* cue so he knows it's okay to drop his head and eat. You have just proven yourself a smart leader who can show him the money. He will think of you as the savvy lead mare and start wanting to follow you anywhere.

NOTE: teach the OKAY and AT EASE cues both verbally and with hand gestures. Another option is to teach a very clear LESSON OVER cue so the horse does not think he did something wrong and you're leaving, ignoring or punishing him for an infraction

## Have fun!

Now that you have the basics of clicker training, you can teach your horse anything you want. Try activities that help you with barn chores or grooming, like sitting in a chair and asking him to move around offering each hoof in turn for cleaning. Teach him to bring you his dinner bucket. Instead of dumping all his feed as a "freebie" ask for behaviors that earn his windfall. Remember to break it down to small steps, then link behaviors to create the final chain. Be generous with your rewards instead of holding out for the entire complete behavior.

There are so many ways to enjoy a horse who's eager to understand you.

Have fun with him!

For questions, ideas, or next steps, contact me anytime at

freelancefreeman@gmail.com
or visit my site at
http://horseclickerfun.blogspot.com

## Happy Trails!

# Acknowledgments, Inspiration & Further Reading

The quick tips you've just read have come from a decade of clicker work, but originated with these wonderful teachers and pioneers in the field of positive reinforcement work.

For more detailed instruction in our pursuit of clicker training, please check out these wonderful experts in the field:

**SHAWNA KARRASH**
You Can Train Your Horse to Do Anything!: Clicker Training and Beyond [VHS]

Shawna Karrasch (Author), Vinton Karrasch (Author), Arlene Newman

**Clicker Training for Your Horse**
**By Alexandra Kurland**

**Karen Murdoch and Lukas**
**http://www.playingwithlukas.com/**
**http://playingwithlukas.com/blog/**

### Peggy Hogan
http://thebestwhisperisaclick.com/
Peggasus@cox.net
http://thebestwhisperisaclick.com/catalog/index.php?main_page=index&cPath=24

### Michelle Dennis
Queensland Australia
http://web.firehorseinspirations.com.au

## Grey Stafford, Ph. D.

Zoomility: Keeper Tales of Training with Positive Reinforcement

http://www.amazon.com/Zoomility-Keeper-Training-Positive-Reinforcement/dp/0979681006

# Various Clicker Types
(all available via PetSmart)

STARMARK Clicker  **$5.99**
http://www.petsmart.com/product/index.jsp?productId=11148557

**Standard Classic Clicker**  **$1.49**
http://www.petsmart.com/product/index.jsp?productId=2751377

**Premier® Clik-R™ Training Tool**  **$5.99**
http://www.petsmart.com/product/index.jsp?productId=11325954&f=PAD%2FpsNotAvailInUS%2FNo

## Taking Notes

Immediately after each session with your horse, jot down some notes so you can chart your progress and consider what to try next time. Better yet, set up a camera to video you and your horse. When you watch it later, you'll be able to see any places where your horse may have gotten stuck as well as your own potential mistakes.

In your notes, include some of these parameters:

- ☐ **Practice Date**
- ☐ **Behavior**
- ☐ **Actions**
- ☐ **Issues to solve**

## PROGRESS NOTES

Printed in Great Britain
by Amazon